101 Great DRINKING Games

Written by
Andrew Studdard
with special thanks to drinking consultant
AnthonyJurist

Illustrated by
Hamish Buchanan and Martin Riskin
Original version ©1992
by **Brewery Products, U.K.**
All Rights Reserved
©1997 by **Boston America Corp.**

30 29 28 27 26 25 24 23 22 21 20 19 18 17 16 15 14

Boston America Corp.

125 Walnut Street, Watertown, MA 02472   (617) 923-1111   FAX: (617) 923-8839

INTRODUCTION

How many times have you been sitting in a bar or at a dinner party and wished the action would liven up? Well this book gives you the chance to really liven events up, wherever you may happen to be. It is an ideal companion to any night out, but you must remember that things tend to get a little out of hand the longer the book is open.

The book is about having a wild night out with games to suit all kinds of occasions and all kinds of people (as long as they are prepared for raucous behavior).

The research needed for this book has taken a number of years and led me into many a dingy bar in the quest for the ultimate drinking game. Each game has been tried and tested several times by a whole bunch of friends, and we have certainly had a lot of fun playing them! I would like to thank all those friends who have helped contribute towards the book and especially Dave Roberts and George Blakeway. A special thanks must go to Hamish Buchanan for the brilliant cartoons in the book, which were produced within a very limited time frame.

Throughout the book I have generally referred to the participants as "he" because using both "he and she" would prove both cumbersome and very awkward. I hope that this does not upset anyone or take anything away from your enjoyment of the book. I hope you all have a fantastic time playing the varied games. Below I have set out a few of the words and expressions used throughout the book, so that you can familiarize yourselves straight away.

The Chairman: This is the person In charge of running the game.

The Chief Sneak: The second in command of the game and it is his job to report to the Chairman any mistakes or bad behavior made during play.

The Judge: A much respected "pillar" of the drinking community. He will be called in if there is a particularly unsavory incident which needs his special judgment.

International Rules: These are the rules which all participants must adhere to during play and they are: 1) left handed drinking only; 2) the Chairman cannot be directly spoken to and he must be approached through the Chief Sneak, using a predetermined sign. If the Chief Sneak makes a mistake, then this is the only time the Chairman may be contacted directly and once again a predetermined sign must be used; 3) no swearing or riotous behavior allowed during play; 4) generally no pointing allowed, except with your elbow.

Fines: These are usually "fingers" of a drink, for example, line your fingers up against the liquid in your glass and drink to the bottom of one, two or three fingers etc.

Boy: "Boy" is another way of being fined and it means that you have to act as a waiter for your friends, plus you have to wear your clothes inside out for the evening.

Note: The author recommends that none of the games in this book are to be played using alcohol because if drunk to excess this can cause loss of balance, slurred speech, double vision, memory loss and I forget what else.

EVENING OPENERS

When they first go out in the evening, most people like to get off to an exhilarating start. This chapter provides a number of games which are short and come straight to the point. They provide many laughs and if they are played for prolonged periods, they can be extremely devastating! You have been warned.

1. Next

Both a simple and quick game which requires two or more people and is an excellent evening opener.

The first player stands up and consumes his glass (which must be full) in one go. When finished he must select another player, point to him and shout "next." This player must then drink his glass, and the game continues until all players have finished their drinks.

It is very unusual to play this game more than two or three times in one evening.

2. The Funnel

You need a large funnel with about a yard-long tube attached to the end of it. One person holds the funnel up in the air, while the person about to drink has the tube ready in his mouth. Then a drink is poured in the top of the funnel and down it goes with no time to think!

Often during this game you can really fix the drinker by having someone continuously pouring liquid into the funnel, which the person drinking generally does not spot—until he feels his bladder about to give way.

3. Fizz Buzz Whizz

A mathematical game which will certainly require a degree of intelligence and therefore it is best to play it before the more raucous behavior starts. Two or more players are required.

Stand or sit in a circle. Player one starts with the words "to my left (or right) 1." The player to his left (or right) responds immediately with "2" and so on around the circle. Sounds simple?

Any number which contains a 3, for example 3, 13, 23, 30, 31, etc., or any number which is a multiple of 3 for example 9, 12,15 etc., the player must say "Fizz." For 5's or multiples of 5, the player must say "Buzz" and for 7's or multiples of 7, "Whizz." For a number such as 15, which is both a multiple of 3 and 5, plus it contains a 5, the player must say "Fizz Buzz Buzz," or in the case of 21, "Fizz Whizz." 35 would be Fizz (contains a 3), Buzz (contains a 5), Buzz (multiple of 5), and Whizz (multiple of 7). So 35 is "Fizz Buzz Buzz Whizz."

An example sequence: 1, 2, Fizz, 4, Buzz, Fizz, Whizz, 8, Fizz, Buzz, 11, Fizz, Fizz, Whizz, Fizz Buzz Buzz, 16 etc...

Any failure to respond immediately with the correct number or word results in that player drinking a fine of his drink. Alternatively that player can take a fine and drop out of the circle until two players battle it out for the win.

This does become easier the more you play the game. When extremely proficient, use any "Whizz" to change the direction of the game.

4. Heads or Tails

This is both a simple and effective game and best played with two or more people. One person flicks a coin and the next person, without looking, has to say if he thinks it is heads or tails. If he predicts wrongly, then he drinks a "finger," but if he is correct, the person flicking the coin drinks. The person flicking the coin will continue until he has flicked against all the participants. This game is best played with small fines because it is a very quick and demanding game which will put you in great voice for the more vociferous games to come later on.

5. Fingers and Toes

This is a game for two people only. You sit on chairs opposite each other with your heels together and your feet pointing out at an angle touching one another.

You each rest a glass on the chair between your thighs, then get a book of matches and, using your forefingers of both hands as pivots, rest the matchbook between the thumbs. Then you must try and flick the matchbook into your opponent's drink. Each time you succeed, your opponent will have to down two "fingers," unless he can get the matchbook into your glass with his next try, which results in four "fingers" to you. The "fingers" keep on accumulating until someone misses.

This can be a very punishing and nerve-tingling game.

6. Indian Poker

You need a group for this game and a deck of cards. One card is dealt to each player and the player must not look at it, but immediately put it on his forehead facing the other participants. Then each person bets a certain number of "fingers." The person with the highest card wins, while the rest have to drink however many "fingers" the winner gambled, plus their own stake (Aces are low in this game). For example, if there are four people playing and the cards facing you are a 4, 5 and 3, then you would have a very good chance of winning. If your card is higher, then everyone drinks the four "fingers" you bet plus their own individual bets as well. A lot of drink may well be consumed if you are too rash with your betting.

7. Hic Hac Hoc

A very quick game best for two people, although three can play.

To play you need to use your hands to make one of three objects; either a stone (clenched fist); a piece of paper (flat palm); or a pair of scissors (index and middle finger pointing out). With these symbols, a stone will blunt scissors, scissors cut paper and paper wraps stone. Whoever is playing puts their fists out in the middle, and then you say "hic hac hoc" and the on the "hoc" you produce one of the above symbols. For example, if there are three people playing and two of them produce scissors whilethe other shows paper, then the two people win and the loser has to drink, because scissors cuts paper. Or if one player produces stone and the other two, scissors, then the first person wins and the other two would play again to see who loses, because stone blunts scissors.

It is also a great game to decide many problems—like who is going to pay for the pizza or who is going to answer the phone, etc.!

LOSE   WIN!

LOSE   WIN!

ALWAYS A WINNER!

8. Luck of the Draw

Begin with a stack of coins set at the table before you. Each person must then predict if the next coin is going to be "heads" or "tails," and every time he is wrong he has to drink two "fingers." The coins will keep on turning until he has predicted the next coin correctly. A short and sweet game which, if your luck is out, can get your evening off to a disastrous start, depending on your views.

9. RUSSIAN ROULETTE

You need six cans of drink and six participants. Shake up one of the cans and place them all in a bag so they are mixed up. One by one take a can out of the bag and open it in front of your face so it is pointing directly at you, and about six inches away. Obviously one of the six will have the shaken can, and it will explode in his face.

Whoever this happens to suffers the indignity of drink all over his face, plus he must then down the remainder in his can.

10. 4 JACKS

An old favorite of every stag night, this simple game is an excellent kick-start to every evening. You require two or more players and a pack of cards.

One player shuffles the cards and proceeds to deal each player one card face up. This continues until a jack is turned up. The player who has received this first jack must choose a drink. The player receiving the second jack must choose a mixer to add to that drink. The third jack means that unfortunate player must pay for the drink, and the final jack spells disaster for that player as he must then consume the beverage.

11. Draw Hic Hac Hoc

This is basically a variation on the normal "Hic Hac Hoc'" (explained earlier), except instead of all throwing your hands out at the same time, you each take turns. You draw your hand out from behind your back first and produce either paper, scissors or stone. Then the other players must try and beat what you have produced.

For example, if stone is drawn, then the winner will be the first to draw paper. If scissors or stone are drawn, instead of paper, then that would automatically mean a drinking fine.

This is a quick-fire game and tends to produce a lot of errors on the draw. Often the participants try to predict the call before it has been made and thus invariably have to drink.

12. Word Association

A simple quick-fire game, but as the evening wears on it inevitably becomes a lot harder. Someone picks an object and the next person has to say a word connected to this object.

For example the word might be "tree" and the next person might say "wood" and then the next person "worm," etc. Any hesitations, obscure connections and stupidity are all punishable by large quantities of drink.

13. Four Heads

The name gives a pretty clear indication of the game. One coin is required and a circle of people. One player will toss the coin, catch it and flick it onto the back of the other hand so that it is still covered (This is not so important early on, but will become clear later.) They then have a look at it; if it is heads they will call "one head" or if it is tails they call "no heads." The coin is then passed on, and any heads gained are added on. When there are three heads, the tension mounts because if the next call is "heads," for example "four heads," the last person to put their hand to their forehead must drink four "fingers."

If this is a bit tame for you, you can add that every time the coin is tossed it must make contact with the roof/ceiling and be caught in the left hand otherwise a fine will be called.

14. OVER AND OUT

This game provides a few laughs because people often think they are a little bit tougher than they actually are. This game sorts out the men from the boys.

You need two barstools and a bottle. You have to rest your ankles on one barstool and your head on the other, so you are fully stretched out. Then you have to see how many times you can pass a bottle over and under your body. This is a hard and tiring exercise to attempt and the winner, the person who does it the most times, fully deserves the drinks that the losers must buy.

15. THE SHOT GUN

All you do here is a simple "hic hac hoc" (explained earlier), to see who goes first. The person who loses gets a can, makes a small hole in the bottom which he covers with his finger, then opens the top of the can making sure his mouth is covering the hole in the bottom. You will soon see and feel the result.

If any spillage results then I am afraid another can must be "shot gunned" until it is consumed perfectly.

16. WHOSE LINE IS IT?

This is a game of improvisation which can be played almost anywhere and during any circumstances.

Pick up an object. Now each person has to think up a use for that object, other than the use for which that object is commonly employed.

For example, you could be at a party and you might stumble across a spoon. We all know that a spoon could be used as a beautiful silver earring or a handy little ear cleaner. Also someone might give you a pencil; how could you improvise? Maybe a suave little pencil thin moustache or a handy conductor's baton, etc.

Anyone who does not show enough imagination has to drink, and anyone too sensible with their ideas should take a fine as well.

17. HIGHER OR LOWER

This is played along the same lines as "Heads or Tails," except that a deck of cards is used. You turn one card over and then have to predict if the next card will be higher or lower. If you are right in your prediction then the game carries onto the next person. If you are wrong then you must take a two "finger" fine and continue until you succeed. If the value of the card turned over is the same as your card, then you automatically lose. Aces are always counted as high.

18. SCRAMBLED EGGS

A game involving two people and a box of eggs.

The two participants each have one egg and stand three paces apart. They then, at the same time, throw the eggs underhand to each other, hopefully catching them. If they succeed, then they take a step back and do exactly the same thing.

Each completed egg throw then results in one step back and two "fingers" of your chosen drink.

This is a very messy but fun game, especially as time wears on.

19. Th Balls Gam

Another strange but brilliant game and best played with about half a dozen people in a crowded place. One person starts by saying "Balls" quite quietly and each person in turn must say "Balls" louder than the person before. Anyone deemed not to have said it louder will be punished by drink.

This game tends to annoy certain sections of a bar/pub and so it is best not to perform it in some cozy little wine bar in the heart of the city unless you wish to leave rather quickly.

"BALLS!"
"BALLS!"
"BALLS!"
"BALLS!"
"BALLS!"
"BALLS!"
"BALLS!"

20. Chase the Ace

A tactical game, easily played at any stage of the evening. The object of the game is to avoid having the lowest card.

One player shuffles the cards and deals one card, face down, to each player. The player to the dealer's left then looks at his card, without showing it to anyone else. If he is sufficiently happy with his card he can elect to keep it (usually if it is over 8); if he is concerned that it is too low, then he can swap his card for the one held by the player to his left. If he elects to swap then he must keep the card he gains from his adjacent player. The next player then has the same options, i.e., either to keep his card or swap with the player to his left. This continues until everyone has had the opportunity to swap, the dealer having no opportunity. The cards are then turned over and the player holding the lowest card must perform the agreed forfeit, for example buying a round, drinking two "fingers," etc. Each player takes a turn to deal so that each person has the opportunity to start.

Aces are low, hence the name of the game, and they tend to be passed right round the table, ending up at the dealer. However, there is one extra rule which can be a lifesaver. If a player holds a king, then he can refuse to swap as the king is unbeatable. This means that a player cannot pass on a low card as he is "blocked" by a player holding a king and he is therefore forced to keep the card he holds.

SET UP GAMES

I didn't think any drinking games book would have been complete without including a chapter on setting people up. Wherever you go there will always be somebody gullible enough to be set up, but the great thing about this section is that all the games are extremely well disguised. As long as everyone plays along, then the victim will not cotton on until it is too late.

All these "Set Up Games" are meant to be lighthearted and the victim will only suffer a tiny bit of humiliation.

21. BOMBER COMMAND

This is a superb set up game involving a large number of people who know the trick and one innocent party who is a little bit naive.

The idea is to pretend you are a B-17 bomber on a mission to bomb "the Hun." Therefore you need four people to act as the propellers on the plane, who sit down on chairs all in a line. You then need a forward gunner and a rear gunner plus a pilot, who all spread themselves along the plane. Then finally you need a "bomb," who is the victim, and he should be sat right in the middle of the plane, so he is sitting between all the participants.

Once everybody is in place the pilot starts the propellers one by one, and thus the people swing their arms around in propeller-like motions. The plane then takes off and everyone involved in the plane leans back in their chairs. Then the plane banks right, so everyone leans right, and then it banks left and so everyone leans left. The pilot then spots enemy aircraft; "Bandits at 2 o'clock" he shouts, and at that point the gunners fire their imaginative guns and make gun-like noises. Suddenly the plane gets hit and the pilot shouts "fire in the bomb bay," and at this point the gunners, the pilot and all those acting as propellers throw their drinks over the bomb in the bomb bay to put the fire out, thus soaking the unfortunate individual. This is a classic game for a packed bar/club and guaranteed to create havoc.

22. THE 3 MAN LIFT

A superb game to play on an unsuspecting person. It is best played in a busy bar.

You need three people who know the trick and one victim. One of the three has to pretend he is really strong and boast to everyone that he is capable of lifting up three people. He then invites the victim to lie flat on his back in front of him, and the other two accomplices to lie on either side, making sure they all interlock arms. Then the so-called "strongman" asks for the victim's belt so he can make sure the attempted lift is totally secure.

With the victim helpless, the "strongman" then grabs a drink and pours it down the victim's trousers and that is the "3 Man Lift." Total humiliation.

PS. The bigger the build up, the better it works. For example, if you go out for an evening with some friends and you wish to play the trick on one of them, then it is best to conspire against one person. This is done by really building up the mystique of the "3 Man Lift" by suggesting that tonight could be the night to attempt it, because you are feeling really strong. Someone is bound to fall for this and then, voila, the trap has been set.

23. THE PARACHUTE JUMP

This is a game to set up an unsuspecting victim. You need two strong men and two trays. The victim, who is the parachutist, stands blindfolded on a sturdy tray. He is told that he will be raised high on the tray, and when he feels his head touch the ceiling he must jump.
The two strong men pick up the tray and raise it waist high and then they drop slowly to a crouching position. At this stage, the parachutist believes he is ascending as he feels them drop beneath him, but really he is only a couple of inches from the ground.
By now he should be having reservations and to scare him a fraction more, it is best to tilt the tray a little or wobble it. Once the tray bearers are at their crouching position, another person then brings a second tray down to rest on the parachutist's head. The parachutist believes he has reached the ceiling so he prepares to leap and take the full force of the drop. Then, as he jumps, it is to much public amusement when he has only jumped two inches or so.

MAB.

24. BLOW FOOTBALL

A great game to set two people up. You need a tray, two straws, a peanut and a lot of water. You get two volunteers who have never seen the game before and a referee. The two volunteers sit opposite each other at a table, and between them is a tray filled with water and a peanut floating in the middle. They figure that it is just a simple game of blow football and so they are all set with their straws poised for action. The referee tells them that on the count of three they must start blowing. Therefore the two volunteers are ready for action and on the count of three, the referee brings his hand down on the tray and completely soaks the two volunteers.

25. The Hands of Fate

The Hands of Fate determine how many "fingers" a person should drink. If someone has been fined or found guilty of doing a stupid caper, then the Hands of Fate can come into operation. The Hands of Fate are a panel of three people who each hold up their hands in a waving motion and when they stop, how every many fingers they are holding up is the fine that person must drink. A little rhyme tends to accompany the Hands of Fate and it goes: "The Hands of Fate, here they go; where they stop, nobody knows." At the end of this rhyme, the victim's fate will be known.

26. Kissing the Blarney Stone

"Blarney" is a castle and town in County Cork, Ireland, and within the castle is what is known as the Blarney stone. This stone is reputed to confer eloquence on those who kiss it. With this in mind, this set up game should take place in a crowded bar or party. To start the game you have to convince the victim about the magical powers of the stone and the honor it will bring to visit it. Once this has been achieved you can begin. The victim is asked to sit on a stool with a blindfold on. First of all he has to fly to Southern Ireland, so that stool is picked up by four people, dragged along the ground (simulating take off), then lifted up and taken around the room finally landing in Southern Ireland with a bump. Throughout all this the victim will be hanging on for dear life. Once he has landed safely he must then embark upon a horse and cart ride to the castle. So once again the stool is shook up, down and around before arriving at the castle. Then he is helped off the stool, still with his blindfold on, and there in front of him is the Blarney stone. At this point you need someone (preferably with a hairy arm), to bend one of their arms, and the victim is then asked to kiss the flesh of the arm just above the elbow. The blindfold is then removed and just at that point you need a man to be walking away pulling up his zipper. Thus the victim believes he has just kissed the man's... and invariably runs out of the pub!

27 BROOM GAME

Equipment needed: One broom, two chairs/tables, and a length of rope, cloth or a soft belt, tied into a small loop (The length of the loop to be approximately two feet). This is an excellent pub trick to be played on an unsuspecting individual. The best way to do this is for an experienced player to go first. The idea of the game is to see how many twists the player can put in the length of rope. Get the player to squat down and place a broom handle behind his knees and in front of his elbows. Then place the loop of rope over his wrists, asking him to clench his fists. Ask the player to see how many times he can twist the rope by revolving one of his wrists. The process will continually shorten the length of rope until no more twists are possible and the wrists are actually almost tied together. As the player twists the rope, get the audience to count, which will encourage him to keep twisting, thus tightening the rope. If the experienced person has gone first, ask a novice to try and beat it. When the novice declares he has beaten the count of the first player, get two experienced players to grab one end of the broom each, and support each end on a table or chair, so leaving the player dangling from the broom. Due to his weight on the loop, he will not be able to move. Leave the player there for sufficient time for everyone to have a good laugh.

28. BANGERS

This game can involve severe pain to the person who has to endure it. You tell the victim that a coin is to be "forced" to stick to his forehead, with the object being to see how many hits on the back of the head it takes to dislodge the coin. You give a demonstration and after a few gentle hits the coin comes off your forehead. The victim will be thinking how easy that all looks, and thus you offer to put the coin on his forehead, pushing it on hard. But really you do not put the coin there at all, taking it away after pushing on it, but to the victim it feels like it is there and he will bang away for some time—until you show him the coin and then he realizes he's been had.

29. THE COURT CASE

The Court Case is the main way of trying a foolish or stupid individual who has committed an offense which is deemed to have gone beyond the bounds of human tolerance. For example, a man might be charged for being a continual pest/deliberate offender during a drinking game, or a man might be charged for deliberately avoiding buying a round of drinks. Once someone is hauled in front of the court, the case is then presided over by a Judge who tends to be a respected member of the drinking community. As well as the Judge there should be a prosecutor and occasionally a defense lawyer, who more than likely will plead guilty for his client anyway. Once all the evidence has been heard, then the jury, normally all those watching the proceedings, will deliver their verdict. This is done by either a thumbs up or a thumbs down sign. Sentence will then be passed by the unbiased Judge. Judges these days tend to be harsh, but fair, but with particularly unsavory individuals they tend to err on the harsh side. If a judge is undecided on the fine to be dished out, then the Hands of Fate can be brought in for the ultimate drinking decision.

30. Th Spoon Gam

Two players are required, one who is in on the trick and the other who is the victim. They must kneel or sit opposite each other and be fairly close with a tablespoon sticking out of their mouths, the handle held in by their teeth. You then explain that in turn each one must bend over forward and allow the other to hit him on the back of the head with the spoon, but only by holding it in their mouths. This continues and the loser is the first to drop out. This would actually carry on for some time as it does not really hurt, but the trick is you have someone with a large ladle standing behind the victim. When the victim's head is down and as the other player brings his spoon down the person with the ladle gives the victim a good crack on the head. The victim obviously thinks it is his opponent and tries to get him back by continuing the game which unfortunately only leads to his further suffering. Great fun for everyone around.

31. Cheeky Cheeky

This is a great set up game involving a large circle with the Chairman standing in the middle giving out the orders. To start with he might say, "touch the cheek of the person on your left with you right hand." In turn everyone does this and says "cheeky cheeky" as they are doing it. The Chairman might then say "touch the nose of the person on your left with your right hand." Once again everyone does this in turn and everyone says "nosey nosey" as they are doing it. This carries on for a number of facial features with the trick being that the person next to the victim dabs his hand in an ashtray every time he does a new command. Thus the victim's face will gradually turn grey. The victim will not realize why everyone is laughing, and to disguise it further the rest of the group must be called into the middle of the circle to drink if they do not put enough feeling into enacting the commands. Once the victim's face has been covered he must then be informed and given a mirror.

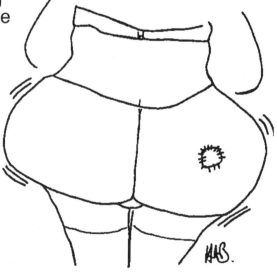

As we all know watching some excellent sport on television, or watching one of the well established soaps is a great way to spend an afternoon or evening, but it can be made more enjoyable by playing drinking games during the proceedings. In this small section I have included a number of games to play while watching the four main groups of sport shown on television, plus I have included a game to play while watching soaps.

32. DRINKING WHILE WATCHING RUGBY/FOOTBALL

In order to play this particular game you write down on individual bits of paper the numbers 1-30 or 1-22 depending on the sport, and these go into a hat to be picked out by the participants of the game.
Then it is simply each time any of your players are mentioned by the commentator you drink a "finger," and if any of your players score, three "fingers" must be consumed. A harsh and exacting drinking game which tends to have dire consequences.

33. DRINKING WHILE WATCHING GOLF

For this game all you have to do is follow one golfer for one hole at a time and predict how many strokes he will take. If you are right then you do not drink, but if you guess incorrectly, then you must drink the difference. For example, if you thought Steve would get a par and he actually bagged a birdie, then a "finger" must be consumed. Or if Jack took a bogey six and you predicted he would get a birdie four, then you would have to drink two "fingers."

34. DRINKING WHILE WATCHING BASKETBALL

This is a game for 2 players, though groups can play also if divided into 2 teams. Each player or group picks a team. As soon as their team gets possession of the ball they must predict whether their team will score or not. If they guess correctly there is no penalty; if wrong, they drink a "finger." This can be a rough game with scores nearing 100 points unless the players have truly inspired guesses.

35. DRINKING WHILE WATCHING SOAPS OR FILMS

This game calls for a little creativity. All the players agree on characters and actions and write them on slips of paper. For example, every time the detective goes into a car or draws a gun or every time a starlet touches her hair. Each player must drink a "finger" or two each time the action occurs. As I said, this game lets you set it up yourself.

36. DRINKING WHILE WATCHING TENNIS

Another simple game which definitely tests your tennis judgment. It is an ideal game to while away those hot balmy days during Wimbledon. All you do is predict who is going to win the next point. If you are right then you do not have to drink, but if you are wrong then a "finger" must be consumed. I would not recommend playing this game for too many sets.

Mass Participation Games

When large groups get together it is important that there are a surplus of games which will bond the group together. This section certainly allows everyone to get involved. It is essential in this section for strong leadership, and so for all you budding Chairmen, now is your chance to take control.

37. Red Indians

This is a game for a large group and is best played at high speed. Each player must think up a stupid/silly sign which he is to be recognized as during the game, and everyone must be told each other's signs. For example your sign might be two fingers up your nose, or two hands on your head, etc. Once these have been established the game can commence. You all sit around a table and drum your two index fingers up and down very quickly on the table, and then the chairman starts by doing his own signal and then randomly someone else's. The person he does then must do his own sign and then another person's. It goes around like this until a mistake is made, which does not tend to be too long, with mistakes being punishable by drink. One rule is that you cannot use the sign of the person who has just nominated you. Finally, the Chairman can at any time shout, "roll call," and this means that everyone in turn must demonstrate their own sign to refresh everyone's memories.

38. Thumper

Another version of the Red Indians Game is called Thumper. Each player selects a silly sign—a fist on his head, a finger slitting a throat, a hand to a nose, a finger in an ear, etc. Each player tries to memorize the others' signs. Play begins with a leader (hopefully someone who has played before) screaming "What's the name of the game?" The group responds, "Thumper!" and then begins a mad frantic pounding on the table with their palms. "And how do you play?" he continues. "You thump!" answers the group. The leader then quickly gives his sign and then the sign of another player. The other player gives the sign of the person he has received the sign from, his own sign and then the sign of the person he wants to "pass" to. And so the game continues amidst loud thumping and yelling. A person breaking the chain, by missing a sign, must finish his drink and then begin the next round.

39. THE TRUTH GAME

This game is best played amongst a close group of friends because it can reveal some rather intimate secrets. One person starts the game by saying something he has never done or somewhere he has never been. For example "I have never read the National Enquirer." All those who have read this quality paper must drink a "finger." All those who deny such an act, but someone remembers seeing them, must drink at least two "fingers." Also, and this is vitally important, if someone boasts of doing something and is actually lying, then he must suffer a severe fine of four "fingers." Lying in any form during a drinking game, is considered a rather heinous offense and you must pay a heavy fine for such transgressions.

40. Wibbly/Wobbly

This is a great game for a large group of people. You need two broom handles and each person must have a full drink. You line up in two teams and when the order is given, the first team member downs his drink and runs to where the brooms are (usually about ten yards away). He then has to put his forehead on top of the broom stick and run round it ten times. Once he has done this, he must try and run back to his team and tag the next member of his team who does exactly the same. The winning side is the first to complete a circuit. Many major problems arise in this game and it is amazing how hard people can concentrate and still not manage to run in a straight line.

41. Pass the Balloon

You fill a balloon with water and then the participants stand in a circle, preferably alternating sexes. The idea is to pass the balloon to the person next to you without using your hands or arms in any way, and without dropping it. The best way of doing this is by lodging the balloon under your chin and then trying to pass it. This can be a tricky maneuver but provides many laughs. Whoever drops the balloon will get soaking wet, plus have to drink a fine.

42. TH TOILET GAM

Can be played with any number of people and is basically a very simple game. You go for a night out and the first person to go to the bathroom becomes "Boy" for the evening. "Boy" basically means that this person has to act as a waiter for everyone else for the whole evening. Within this role he also has to wear his clothes inside out, which includes wearing his underwear outside his pants and his tie around his head, just to bring further humiliation upon the poor soul. It is a harsh penalty and so beware: keep those legs crossed!

43. COMMANDER

This is definitely a game for a large group of people and is a game based on "Simon Says." Everyone sits in a circle with the palms of their hands out in front. Before the game starts, the Commander, who should be somebody very proficient at the game, is selected. Also a "Chief Sneak" should be chosen. This should be somebody who is relatively sharp, as it is his job to spot any mistakes made. The game is best played around a large table and the game starts once the Commander says "game on." From this point forward, everyone must be quiet. Then everything the Commander says which is prefixed with the word "commander," must be followed by the participants. For example, the Commander might say "Commander biblibobs," which is when you move the fingers of your hands up and down quickly. Then the Commander might say "Commander high," so you would raise your hands up. He then might say "Commander Lo" and then you lower your hands, so your fingers are pointing to the floor. All this should be done very quickly and the Commander may continue doing this a few times and suddenly say a command without "commander" before it, and anyone caught disobeying will be punished, usually by a small fine. As well as "biblibobs" and "high" and "low," the Commander should use other commands like "high biblibobs," which are arms raised and hands biblibobbing; Commander "very high," when you all stand up and raise your hands high; Commander "even higher," when you stand on a chair and once again raise your hands.

Other suggested actions include: "Commander surfing" — all stand on chairs and pretend you are surfing; "Commander canoeing" — same as above but paddling; "Commander swimming" — same as above but swimming. A great one to use to liven things up are songs. For example, "Commander *Hawaii-Five-O*" means you sing the theme to this show and simulate swimming and canoeing actions. "Commander *American Pie*" — you sing the chorus of *American Pie*. There must be silence during the game with only the Commander allowed to speak. If a mistake is made and the Chief Sneak spots it, then he tells the Commander who dishes out the fine. If the Chief Sneak does not spot the mistake but one of the players does, then that person may address the Chief Sneak using a predetermined signal, like right hand on head or two fingers up your nose. The Chief Sneak will then tell the Commander, and the fine will be dished out. The Commander may only be directly addressed if the Chief Sneak makes a mistake and, probably to general public clamor, the Chief Sneak should be treated severely. Finally, if the Commander fails to catch someone out during a single go then he must voluntarily drink. Good Luck.

44. THE JUG GAME

You need a jug filled with a suitable liquid and a large number of people. To start playing, you pass the jug around the circle with each person drinking as little or as much as he likes directly out of the jug. Sounds fairly simple? Well, the object is to get someone to buy the next jug. This can only occur when one person finishes off the jug and then it is the person who has the penalty drink (the drink before the one that emptied the jug) who must buy the next one. Therefore as you can see it is a fairly tactical game, because if there is about one fifth of the jug left, you must decide whether to finish this off or risk whether the next person in line will do so or not. If that person finishes it off then you would have to buy the next jug.

45. PUB GOLF

You need a town with a number of pubs and a large group. You then designate your route with each pub being one hole. Each pub is a Par 3 which means you have three attempts to down your drink. A lot of people like to go for holes in one at every pub. This is very commendable, but can you come unstuck later on? Also, every time you go to the toilet you lose a stroke or a lot more if you are playing "The Toilet Game" (Explained above). In at least two of the pubs you must have a chaser to go with your drink, and these pubs are rated Par 4. It is best to have a score card for yourself, with the winner having the lowest score, and the prizes should be worked out beforehand. Generally prizes should be of the liquid variety and plenty of it.

46. ALIENS

A game which definitely requires a sense of humor and a shedding of any inhibitions. You all sit in a circle facing each other. One player is elected to start, he then must perform an impression of an alien life-form, with facial and physical impressions as well as a suitable noise. After a short period of time, which is determined by the impressionist, he must stop all actions and immediately point to another player in the circle who must instantaneously begin his impression. Again, after a period he stops and points to another player and so the game continues. The Chairman must allocate fines for: a) any hesitation by players, b) any impressions which are deemed to be too similar to previous impressions and c) any player not giving a 100% performance.

Note: - This game is guaranteed to annoy Bartenders to the extent that most games result in the removal of all players to another pub.

47. Bunnies

This is a game for a large group of people. To play this game you must know how to do a simple "bunny" which is done by putting your thumbs on your temples and wiggling your fingers about. To do a "half bunny," you use one hand to do the wiggling. You start the game by doing general "hovers" which are arms out and fingers moving up and down. Then the Chairman points at another player, and that player must do a "bunny" motion, and the players on either side must do a "half bunny" motion according to which side the main "bunny" is. For example, if you are sitting to the right of the "bunny," then you do a "half bunny" with your left hand which is your thumb on your left temple and fingers wiggling. The player who is the "bunny" has to point at someone else to make that person "bunny." He does this by taking his hands off his temples and pointing with his fingers. To add spice to the game the person who is "bunny" is allowed to fake his pointing once per go, but his hands must not come off his temples when doing this. If anyone falls for a dummy then they drink and if anyone fails to do a "half bunny," then they drink. The Chairman must keep a firm grip on the proceedings.

48. SLAPS

A game which keeps everyone thinking and can be played with any number of people. To start, everyone must sit around a table and place their hands flat on the table with their arms interlinked. The person who starts states the direction of play and slaps one hand down on the table. The next person then has to slap and so on in that direction without hesitation. This continues until someone either slaps twice, three, four or five times. For example: a double slap changes the direction of the play; a triple slap means continuing in the same direction but jumping one hand; a quadruple slap means everybody has to stand up and take a drink, left handed drinking, of course; a fifth slap means that everybody must stand up and sing a line from a predetermined song, such as *Hotel California* by the Eagles. There are various fines for mistakes/hesitation, and you should gradually increase the speed of the game.

49. KNIGHTS, CASTLES, PRINCES

This is a game for a large number of people and definitely needs male/female participation. This game requires one Chairman shouting out the commands which are as follows: "Knights" - The man lifts the woman in cradle fashion. "Castles" - The man gives the woman a piggy back. "Princes" - The woman straddles the man. These are the basic commands, and once everyone is familiar with these, then everyone must pair off and the game can commence. Music is played and everyone walks around in a large circle until the music stops, then the Chairman shouts one of the three commands. If a couple does the wrong command then they are out and have to drink a fine. If everyone does the right command then the last pair to complete it drops out and drinks. Often the competitors tend to collapse during the game due to either the weight of the lady partner or just general laughter. Thus it is fairly easy to distinguish who has come last. The game is played until there is only one couple left, thus they are the winners and become "King and Queen" for the night.

50. ANIMAL FARM

This is a game for a large number of people and requires an imaginative chairman, who is able to make up a story as he goes along. Each participant takes the name of a farmyard animal, then the chairman begins telling the story and mentioning the names of the different animals. Each time a person's farmyard animal is mentioned, he must make the noise of his animal and then drink one "finger;" but if he forgets, he must consume double the amount. Every time the chairman utters the words "the farmyard," everyone must make their animal noises in unison and then drink a "finger."

51. BULLSHIT

This game is best played with a large number of people because this will result in mass confusion. Each person selects an animal and tells everyone the animal chosen. It is important to remember everybody's animal name otherwise it could be costly. The game is started by the Chairman shouting out one of the animal names plus "shit." For example, "sheepshit." Then the person whose animal was used replies "bullshit." The Chairman replies with "whose shit?" and the other person says another animal name. For example, say there is a cat, cow, dog, and goose. If the person who is the cow says "dogshit" then the person who is a dog replies "bullshit." The cow replies "whose shit?" and the dog must say another animal, such as "gooseshit." The person who is a goose then must reply "bullshit" and the dog says "whose shit?" and the goose says another animal name, etc. One rule is you cannot repeat the animal name you are conversing with. This game is best played at high speed because then mistakes are made much more frequently. Any crass mistakes, like replying with the wrong response, hesitation, or using an animal name which does not exist results in a large drinking fine of normally between two and four "fingers."

52. Boat Race

An old favorite of many an evening and a game for as many people as possible, but you must have equal numbers on each side. You have two teams who line up facing each other, preferably pairing off against one another. Each player has a large drink and the game is started at one end with two opposing team members downing their drinks. Once they have finished, they must put their empty glasses on their heads and the next person begins. Obviously the winning side is the one that downs its drinks the quickest. It is then usually etiquette for the losers to buy the winners a drink or to have a rematch.

53. SPIN THE BOTTLE

A very simple traditional drinking game and can be played with as many people as you want. All you do is put a bottle in the middle of the table/ floor and spin it. Whoever the bottle points to has to drink a fine or take a swig out of the bottle you are spinning. A good hearty spin must be enacted every time, otherwise accusations of cheating will be flying around and this would inevitably prove extremely costly to the person concerned.

54. BLINDFOLD GAME

You split into two teams and at one end of the room there is a table with a drink on it for each member of the team. One member of each team is blindfolded and turned around ten times. They then have to try and get to the table and down their drink. Once this has been safely negotiated, they return to their team and hand the blindfold to the next person, who attempts to do exactly the same. All sounds fairly simple? Well, the trick to this game is teamwork, in that one member of the team must direct the person who is blindfolded, otherwise chaos will reign. The losing team must buy the winners a drink. Warning: This game often results in breakages and accidents.

55. RATS

Best played with a large group. Each player gets a bottle top/cap, makes a hole in it, puts a long bit of string through the hole and ties it on. All the bottle tops or "Rats" are placed tightly in the middle with the participants holding the strings at the edge of the table. One person, who is known as the "catcher," does not have a "Rat" but has a cup/bowl just large enough to fit over all the "Rats" when they are placed in the middle. He holds the cup face down at the edge of the table and the object is to catch as many of the "Rats" as possible while they are still in the middle. The catcher counts down "three, two, one, go." Every time he catches one, that person has to drink four "fingers" then drop out, and every time he fails to catch one he has to drink a "finger." Basically the people holding the strings, who will be crouching at the edge of the table, have to pull them away as quickly as possible so that their "Rats" are not caught, otherwise they must face the consequences. Anyone deemed to be pulling their "Rat" away too early must drink the four "finger" fine and still remain in the game. This game tends to get a little bit violent and aggressive especially as the evening wears on. The catcher must be changed once he has caught all the "Rats."

56. FLEXIBLE FRIENDS

This is a bit of a personal game and is most fun when played with men and women, sitting alternately around a table. Someone donates a credit card and you have to pass it to the person on your left using your mouth only, with the catch being you have to suction it on your lips in order to pass it. Basically the card has to be flat against your lips, and passing occurs with one person sucking while the other is blowing. If the card is dropped, the consequence is a stiff fine for both the passer and receiver. Many awkward positions tend to unfurl themselves during this game, which makes it extremely amusing.

57. STRAW BOAT RACE

This is basically the same as a normal "Boat Race" except that each participant uses a straw. It is best played with an equal number of people on each side. Plenty of encouragement is required from team members because it tends to be a slow and hazardous procedure, but you will feel exhilarated once you have achieved it. Once again the losers should buy the winners a drink. Warning: It is not advisable to play this game too many times in an evening.

58. MATCHBOX GAME

This is a game preferably for a large group of people. You need a matchbox, a drink each and a decent-sized table so that everyone can sit around it. The object is to throw the matchbox over your drink so that it lands on the table. If it lands on its side, then the next person in line has to drink two "fingers." If it lands on its end, then four "fingers;" and if it lands flat then it is nothing. For example, if the matchbox is thrown on its side then it is two "fingers" to the next person in line, and if he throws it flat then he has to drink the four "fingers." Basically the "fingers" accumulate until someone fails with a throw. If the matchbox is thrown into one of the glasses, then the thrower will have to drink all his drink. If the matchbox is thrown off the table, then the thrower will once again have to drink the lot. Beware of playing this game with a large jug in the middle of the table, because if the matchbox ends up in the jug, then the thrower will have a lot of drinking to do.

59. Airports

This is an excellent idea for a party or a bar/pub crawl and an infinite number of people can play. Everyone forms a conga line with the Captain at the front. When everyone is settled you move off to a room in the house or a pub/bar. Each room or pub represents an airport of a country around the world and in each country you visit everyone must consume a drink representative of the country. Once this has been negotiated you all, in the conga fashion, fly onto the next destination, and therefore a global pub crawl is undertaken. The more countries you visit, the more likelihood there is of a touch of turbulence and so the Captain has to keep a sharp eye on his crew and passengers for any who fall out or experience travel sickness.

60. Naughty Words

A very unusual game and can be played with as many people as you want. It is very simple; all you do is for short periods of the evening, say fifteen minutes of every hour, each person playing must end their sentence with a certain rude/obscene word, and if this is not adhered to then you must take a fine. For example your word might be 'prick' and you might be chatting to someone who is not in the game and you must end your sentence with the word. For example, "Bartender, can I have five pints and two bags of chips, thanks, prick." This can be pretty embarrassing, but if you do not do it, then a severe penalty must be taken.

61. Tin Can Basketball

The players are divided into two teams and separated by about 15 feet. A tin wastepaper basket or a trash can is placed in front of each group. Cases of canned beverages should be available to each team. The players drink a can as quickly as possible and then pitch the empty into the opposite basket, which makes a lot of noise at it hits the tin. The game continues until the cans or players run out, or a time limit of 8 minutes is reached. The team whose target basket contains the most cans wins. This game is particularly suited for playing on a patio or deck.

DARTBOARD GAMES

Darts originated in Britain but millions of people throughout other countries play the game regularly. I have included in this section a handful of games which will really spice up your darts evening and provide many hours of entertainment.

62. NEAREST THE EDGE OF THE DARTBOARD

This is best played with a fairly large number of players. You try to get as near to the edge of the board as is possible without going off it. If you go off the board you automatically drink. The rules are that the person who is nearest the edge chooses the drink and the person furthest away or off the board has to drink it. Often it is best to play it a little bit safe because there is always some clown who tends to miss the board.

63. Killer

The more people the merrier for this game. You each throw a dart with your left hand to decide your number. You then have to hit your number five times to become a killer, with a "double" counting as two and a "triple" as three hits. Once you are a killer you can hit the other players' numbers and knock them down. To totally destroy someone you have to hit them down to minus one. If you hit your own number while you are a killer then you lose one. Basically once you are knocked out you drink and the winner is the last person left in.

64. Man for Man Darts

Each player has three darts and a number is decided upon which you all go for. The person who hits the number the least will take a fine. The fines are worked out by splitting the difference of the person who scored the most with the person who scored the least. For example if "twenties" were the required number and the winner managed four of them, while the last placed person managed only one, then he would consume three "fingers" (the difference between the two scores). Warning: Do not play this game if you are a beginner because your game will not improve.

65. Golf Darts

You play 18 holes using the numbers 1-18 on the board. A triple of the number you are going for is a hole in one; a double is a birdie and the section between the triple and the Bull is a par. The section between the triple and the double is a bogey one over par, hitting the Bull is also a one over par and anywhere else on the board is a triple bogey six. On this game it is best to take your fines after each hole, for example one, two, three "fingers." If you get under par then you accumulate minus "fingers."

GAMES WHICH RUN THROUGHOUT THE EVENING

Whenever you play drinking games it is always satisfying to be able to get back at another member of your group. This section will enable you to do just that and all the games included will make your evening an eventful one and hopefully enable you to have the last laugh.

66. WATCHDOG

This game keeps everyone awake throughout the whole evening with the people suffering tending to get a little wearisome as proceedings unfold. The game is started in a haphazard manner with someone placing a coin in another person's drink. This spells the beginning of the game and marks the start of open warfare. The unfortunate individual with the coin now in his drink must consume what is in front of him, making sure that he collects the coin between his teeth as he finishes the last drops of his drink. Then, at any time during the evening he can try and place the coin in someone else's drink. If he succeeds, then they consume, but if he loses the coin in an attempt to get someone else, then he once again must drink.

67. COMPULSORY CARDS

These are ideal accompaniments to a ski, football, roadtrip tour or to any large groups of people. Any kind of cards are handed out to everyone in the group, and you normally give each person three cards for the duration of the trip. Then a card can be played at any time during the trip and whatever is suggested must be done or face a very heavy fine, which must be a predetermined one. Some typical suggestions are: Compulsory "down in ones." Compulsory "dead ants," for example everyone lies on their backs with feet and arms waving in the air like a dead ant. Compulsory singing. Compulsory lying.

68. Odd One Out

A simple but effective game and one to play when everyone is not expecting it. What you do is, if you are sitting with a group of friends, one person, who may be feeling a bit bored, will suddenly stand up and say "one," then someone else must individually stand up and say "two" and then another person "three," etc. But two people must not stand up at the same time or they have to down the rest of their drink and the last person to stand up out of the whole group drinks a three "finger" fine.

69. Pin It

This game is best played with a large group of people and should be played at all sorts of social gatherings like stag night, banquets, wedding receptions, etc. You play using a clothes pin. The object of the game is for one person to attach the clothespin to someone else without that person knowing about it. Then someone very loudly shouts "Pin it" and everyone in the room quickly checks themselves for the pin and there is a ten second time limit to do so. If the clothespin is not found on the person's body then he will have to drink what he has got in front of him. If the pin is found, then the person who shouted "Pin it" has to drink. If the person is caught attaching the pin by the man he is attempting to put it on, then he has to drink. Finally if the pin drops off before "Pin it" is called, then once again the person who attached the pin drinks. It is best to pin someone who has just bought a fresh drink because then, if you succeed, he will shortly be visiting the bar again.

70. BURP GAME

This game carries on throughout the evening and so everyone must always be on their toes. It is very simple in that every time a member of the group happens to burp, everyone must put one of their hands on their forehead. Anyone who does not remember to do this, automatically gets a good hard slap on the forehead from all members of the group. It is very unsportsmanlike to let out a burp on purpose and anyone thought to be doing so can either be hauled in front of the judge, or made to take an automatic drinking fine. You have been warned.

71. THE HERSHEY KISS GAME

This game tends to be one of those which keeps recurring throughout the evening, thus keeping everyone on their toes. The game commences when someone manages to get a Hershey Kiss in your drink. You then have fifteen seconds to get it out using only your tongue and teeth, while everyone else is counting down. No hands are allowed whatsoever. If you succeed, you eat the Kiss, but if you fail, you have to down your drink plus the chocolate. The victim then is given a fresh Kiss for his revenge on anyone in the group, so beware!

GAMES FOR SMALLER GROUPS

Often an evening is spent with just a few of your friends and a quiet, polite evening develops. This section will change all that. It is aimed at smaller groups, for example, between two and twelve people. The games included will add a different meaning to the term "a quiet night out." Raucous behavior will certainly ensue and laughter will be aplenty.

72. QUARTERS

Best played with three or more people. All the players sit around a table with glasses of drink. The drinks are all tightly bunched in the middle of the table, with an extra glass right in the middle. The object is to bounce the coin on the table and then have it bounce into another person's glass. If you are successful, then that person drinks. If you get the coin in your own glass then you drink. If you succeed in getting it in the middle glass then everyone must down their drink and the last person to finish drinks the middle one as well. If the coin is bounced off the table then the guilty party has to consume. This game can take a little practice.

73. SPOOF

Most definitely a "gentleman's" game with no "sloppy" behavior allowed. Best played with four to six players although any number can play. Three coins are required by each player and after holding them behind your backs you hold out one fist with either 0,1,2, or 3 coins in it. The idea is to guess the total number of coins in all the fists. For example, with six players, the calls will be between 0 and 18. Everyone gets to make a guess, but they all must be different. Once everyone has made their call, the fists are opened and the coins added up. The person who made the correct guess is out. If, however, the winner displays such inappropriate behavior as cheering or raising a fist, then he is back in the game. The game is repeated until only two players are left for a head to head to decide the ultimate loser, who should have a hefty drinking fine of normally four "fingers" or more. This game is strictly a "gentleman's" game and therefore no cheating or false calling is allowed. An example of this behavior would be if you had 2 coins in your fist and you guess a total number of 1. This is deemed ungentlemanly behavior because it is a false call and should receive the necessary punishment.

74. TICKLED PINKIES

This game sorts out the men from the boys and the women from the girls. Only people with very ticklish feet are allowed to participate in this game. The object of the game is to see how long you can "hold out" while your feet are being intensely tickled by as many as three people! It is best to sit on a comfy chair with one foot on a "tickling" stool. You need a stop watch to time your endurance. The winner having the best time, while the losers suffer the further punishment of a stiff drinking fine. Caution: Many tears will be shed.

75. FUZZY DUCK

This is a favored game of many a drinking community, basically because chaos is bound to set in. You all sit around a table and one person states the direction he wants to go and says "fuzzy duck." The next player repeats "fuzzy duck" and so on until one player decides to say "does he." (Note: anyone can say this). From then on the words "ducky fuzz" must be repeated until someone says "does he" again, which is when the words get swapped back to the original "fuzzy duck." This might all sound pretty straight forward, but both "fuzzy duck" and "ducky fuzz" are both very similar sounding, and once the slurring stage of the evening is upon you, all types of problems will occur. Large drinks should be consumed for general mistakes, swearing and nervous breakdowns.

76. RISING SUN

This is a verbal version of "Slaps" (Game #48), but played with an Oriental emphasis. The rules are, if you say "Yip" then the play starts in the direction you indicate; "Yong" changes the direction; "Yang" goes the same way but misses one person; "Ying," you all stand up and drink a "finger;" finally "Yeng" means that you all stand up and sing the chorus from that classic Vapours' song of 1980, *Turning Japanese*, or anything from *The Mikado*. All these calls are to be done at high speed with drinking penalties for hesitation, mispronunciation and calling when it is not your call.

77. OBSTACLES

This game is not for the faint-hearted and basically requires four or more people. To play you need three glasses, two dice and a counter. The glasses are spaced out in a line with each glass being filled with different amounts of liquid. The first player rolls the dice and he has to say if he thinks he will roll higher or lower with his next throw. Whatever he says will determine the sequence of high or low to come. For example, if he throws a 6 to start off with, he will obviously call lower. A 5 might then be thrown and he will move past the first glass, not having to drink. But on his next roll, the die must be higher than 5, due to the sequence high/low. He can only move on until a 6 is thrown and each time he fails to achieve this he has to drink, with the glass obstacle being filled up to the same level each time he makes a mistake. Once the three drinks have been successfully negotiated you have the choice of either attempting to renegotiate the "obstacles," or to drink all three glasses...a tricky decision!

78. TEN GUESSES

You pick a sport or subject like cinema, football, or politics and then one person in the group has to think of a famous person within that category. The people playing then have ten "free" yes-or-no-questions to ask to determine the identity of the person. If the person's name is not found after ten questions, then every question asked after that is one "finger" of a drink. If the famous person is guessed before ten questions are asked, then the guy thinking of the person must drink, in "fingers," number of questions asked deducted from ten. For example, if four guesses are taken then he must drink six "fingers."

79. MY OLD GRANDMA

This is a game of memory and repetition. You start the game by saying "my old grandma went down the market and bought a basket of ..." (for example "apples"). Then the next person must say "my old grandma went down the market and bought a basket of apples and..." then add another item, for example, "pears." Therefore each person has to add on an extra item, but you also must remember to repeat what has been said before. If any items are not repeated you must drink at least two "fingers" for every item missed.

80. Touch Too Much

Can be played with two or more people, preferably a slightly larger group. You need a sheet of tissue paper, an elastic band and a glass. Place the tissue paper over the glass and attach it using the elastic band. Then place a coin in the middle of the tissue. With a lit cigarette, take turns burning holes in the tissue paper, trying not to let the coin drop into the glass. The person who burns the hole which drops the coin is the loser and then downs a drink. This game can turn into a very tactical affair because the risk takers amongst you will burn holes close to the coin and thus dramatically increase the problems for the next person.

81. SING A SUBJECT

This is a game guaranteed to liven up proceedings as long as everyone puts all their effort into it. A Chairman picks a certain subject. Everyone then has to think of a song with that subject contained within it and then sing a line from that song. For example, you might choose the category "colors" and what springs to mind could be Elvis Presley's *Blue Suede Shoes*. Another example might be the Chairman choosing "food" and thus someone might choose Jimmy Buffet's *Cheeseburger in Paradise* or The Beatles' *Strawberry Fields*. Everyone in the group must think of a song or face dire consequences. Fines should be dished out for unconvincing singing or failure to think of a song. Once everyone has become proficient at singing one line from a song, you then must try and sing a whole verse, and major problems will definitely result.

82. HARRY

Get in a circle. The first person starts it off by looking at a member of the group and saying to that person, "Harry." Then that person will reply "yes, Harry," and the first person says, "tell Harry." Then that person continues with exactly the same lines on another person in the group. If someone mucks it up, then they immediately become "Harry one spot." The second person to muck it up becomes "Harry two spot," etc. After it has been around the group a few times the game should be speeded up, plus you should all swap seats, and then real confusion sets in.

Basically a great game for three or more of you. What you need to know in this game is that to go to the left you hit the left part of your chest with your right fist and to go to the right you hit the right part of your chest with your left fist. Someone starts by going right or left and then the next person can carry on in the same direction or reverse the direction. When it gets to the fifth person he then holds his hands above one another so that the fingers are pointing sideways and which ever way the top hand's fingers are pointing is the way it goes. For example, if your right hand is on top of your left then the direction will be to the left. When it reaches seven, the seventh man points at another player and then it starts from one again. It is basically a game going from numbers one to seven and just continues going around. It sounds very simple but most of the simple games tend to create havoc. Make drinking fines for hesitation and stupidity.

84. SINKING GLASS

What you need for this game is a glass and a jug of water. You float the glass in the jug of water and then take turns to put as much/little water in the floating glass as you like, with the person who makes it hit the bottom losing. Large fines should be dished out for the losers and you must remember that you should not be too rash when putting the water in the glass because some glasses sink rather quickly.

85. THE SLAPPING CLAPPING CLICKING GAME

You start this game by doing general hovers with both hands (for example biblibobs, where you move your fingers up and down, explained earlier), then the Chairman shouts "drop them." Everyone first slaps their thighs, then claps, then snaps the fingers of their right hand and then their left hand and this is the routine for the whole game, so it is best to learn it quickly. You must remember that you can only speak on the snapping of the fingers and at no other time. The Chairman will then say "give me," but this can only be said on the snapping of the fingers; then "names of" (only on the finger snapping); "famous people" (only on the finger snapping); 'to my left," (only on the finger snapping); "Robin Williams," and then the next person must continue, etc. Fines are given for speaking any time other than the finger snapping, forgetting the sequence of slapping, clapping, snapping, or not thinking of a name when it is your turn. Also any subjects can be used and the harder the better. Some suggested topics are: types of drink, famous models, makes of condoms, etc. As you get better at this game it is best to speed things up; then more mistakes are made, and thus more drinking.

86. GIRAFFES

All you need to play is a matchbox. You start by someone kneeling down with their hands behind their back. While in this position he must try, by bending forward toward the ground, to pick up the inside of an empty matchbox, which has been placed on the floor in front of them, using only his nose and without toppling over. If everyone achieves this then the matchbox is moved a little further away. If a person topples over then he must drink a fine of three "fingers" and then drop out. The winner is the person who manages the furthest distance without toppling over.

87. CARDINAL PUFF

This game is best played with a small group and each participant must be very observant and alert at all times. Everyone sits around a table and the Chairman starts the game by standing up with his full glass and announcing, "I drink to the health of Cardinal Puff." He then sits down, places his glass on the table, taps the table with one finger of his left hand and then one finger of his right hand. He then taps the underside of the table once with one finger of each hand. Then he taps his right leg with his right hand once and his left leg with his left hand once. He then picks up his glass, holding it with one finger and his thumb, takes one sip and taps the glass down once on the table. He then says, "I drink to the health of Cardinal Puff for the second time." Then he repeats the above sequence, tapping the table twice with two fingers, tapping the underside of the table twice with two fingers, tapping both his legs twice and then holding his glass with two fingers and the thumb and finally placing the glass down twice. Then he announces, "I drink to the health of Cardinal Puff for the third and final time." Everything is done as above but three times and with three fingers, and once this has all been done, he sits down and the next person must try his luck at drinking to the Cardinal's health. Any mistakes result in that person drinking a fine and starting again. It can be a long and difficult process for many people!

TAP!
TAP!

88. CONCEAL THE COIN

This game is best played with six people. You need two teams of three who sit opposite each other. You decide who is to go first. One team has the coin and all their hands go under the table and then the coin is transferred to one of the six hands. When the coin is passed, they simultaneously bring their hands flat down on the table and the opposing side will have to guess which hand contains the coin. Often, when the hands are slapped down on the table, the noise of the coin hitting the table can give a major clue. If the coin is found in one guess, the hiding side has to drink three "fingers." In two guesses, two "fingers." For three guesses both sides drink one "finger" and with four, five or six guesses, the guessing side drinks two, three and four "fingers."

89. IBBLE DIBBLE

This is a game for a maximum of twelve people with each of the players having a number, from one to twelve or whatever. Then the person who is "Ibble Dibble number one," for example says: "This is 'Ibble Dibble number one,' with no Ibbles or Dibbles, calling 'Ibble Dibble number six,' with no Ibbles or Dibbles, Ibble Dibble." Any mistakes in the above wording, the number of Ibble Dibbles a player has, or undue hesitation will result in a player acquiring an Ibble Dibble, which is a mark placed on the face with the burnt end of a cork. The player must also consume three "fingers." Therefore each mistake made results in an Ibble Dibble. You must then remember how many Ibble Dibbles you have and how many everyone else has and use these numbers when calling and reporting, otherwise chaos reigns. This game usually ends up with numerous participants covered in cork marks due to absolute mayhem.

90. Armchair Tunnels

This game was discovered in an Officers' Mess in Germany where this peculiar sport appeals to those with definite aggressive tendencies. Place at least six chairs on their backs with the legs against each other so that they form a tunnel shape. Two players compete against each other and the remainder of people present sit on the backs of the chairs, thus stopping any of the chairs moving. The two players start at opposite ends of the room and the winner is the first player through the tunnel to touch the other end of the room. The result is, of course, a certain amount of "foul play" in the tunnel to prevent your opponent from getting through before you. There are no rules and the loser has to buy the victorious opponent a drink.

91. Peanuts

This is best played with two or more people. The game requires each participant to have a large fizzy drink and a salted peanut. Each participant drops his nut into his drink. It should then drop to the bottom, and the first person's peanut to float to the top is the winner. The losers will then have to consume their drinks. Experience will count in this game, because you will soon realize that the type of nut used is extremely important, for example dry roasted or ready salted. Also what liquid you are using to race your nut in is crucial. You have been warned.

92. Follow My Leader

Each person has to follow what the "Leader" says. Basically it is a little song with a new line added every time it goes around the group. The song goes like this:- One red hen. Two cute ducks. Three brown bears. Four running hares. Five fat females sitting sipping scotch smoking cigarettes. Six sleazy sluts slinking and sliding in slippery snow. Seven elongated alligators eating anteaters. Eight enormous elephants escalating elevators. Nine naughty nuns nuzzling naughty Nicki's nighties. The Leader starts by saying the first line and each individual in turn has to repeat this. Then the Leader says the first and second lines and everyone in turn must repeat what has been said. It continues on like this, so each time a new verse is added, all the previous verses must be spoken as well. As you can see, as the song goes on it gets a little bit more complicated as each verse unfolds. Many mistakes are made, so much drinking will be done. This game has a simple equation: the more you drink, the more mistakes you make, and mistakes mean more drinks.

93. Dambusters

A good, simple but hilarious "family" drinking game. Put a large filled glass about ten feet away on the floor and take turns trying to drop five coins in the glass all in one go. It sounds easy, but all the coins must somehow be held between your thighs, so you are still able to walk and then aim at your target. Each person always has a different technique and the consequences tend to be hilarious. All the coins must go in and so it can take a number of attempts to achieve this. The last person to drop his coins in, has to drink what is in the glass.

94. ZOOM

The idea of Zoom is to pass an imaginary ball around the circle by making eye contact with another player and saying one of the following three words. "Zoom" is the most basic, where you pass the ball (control) to the person you are looking at. "Swartz" is what you say if you want to pass the ball (control) straight back to the person who passed it to you. You look at that person and say, "Swartz." "Befidiliano" is the trickiest call of all. This is when you want to pass the ball back to the person that passed it to you, but you look at someone else and say, "Befidialiano." This will probably trick the person that passed it to you, since you are not looking at him when you pass it back, as well as trick the person you are looking at, since he will want to respond. Confusion always sets in and two "finger" fines should be readily consumed for any mistakes.

95. CRISS-CROSS

Here's a simple game if a group of you are sitting around. Each person must be addressed by the name of the person on the right for a set period of time, or alternatively you can each take the name of a famous person and have to be addressed by that name for the set period of time. Any mistakes on names means a fine.

96. BLOWING IN THE WIND

A game for a number of people. All you need is a deck of cards and an empty glass. You place the deck of cards on top of the glass and you take turns trying to blow cards off the pack using only one breath per turn. You must blow a minimum of one card off per turn, otherwise you drink. If you blow all the cards off the glass, then you also lose and take a four "finger" fine. If only one card is left on the glass then the person whose turn it is will automatically lose and suffer the indignity of having to consume six "fingers."

97. FROGS

Best played with four or more people and fairly late on in the evening. The chairman says "one frog, two eyes, four legs, plop into the pond." The second person says "two frogs, four eyes, eight legs, plop, plop into the pond." It carries on accumulating until someone makes a mistake, or someone is too slow with their turn. This might all sound rather simple, but I can assure you that major problems always occur and a blankness often envelops your mind as the game rolls on. Every mistake should mean at least a two "finger" fine, if not more.

98. DRINK WHILE YOU THINK

This game is best played with two or more people. Decide on a topic, such as famous movie stars. One person will start drinking his drink until he has thought of a name in this category. He then says that name and the next person continues by using the first letter of the surname to start the Christian name of another famous movie star. Confused? For example, if one person said Clint Eastwood, then the next person would start with the letter "E" and say a name like Emma Thompson, and remember all the thinking is done while you are consuming your drink. There is a slight catch to this game because if a name is said where the Christian name and surname start with the same letter, then the direction changes. For example, if someone says Marilyn Monroe, which both the Christian name and surname start with an "M," the direction changes. Some suggested topics are: famous athletes, famous musicians, famous politicians.

99. Hi Ho

To play this game you must know the tune and words of "Hi Ho." This goes, "hi ho, hi ho, it's off to work we go, with a shovel and a pick and a walking stick, hi ho, hi ho hi ho, hi ho, hi ho it's off to work..." etc. Once this is known you each get two glasses/bottles and hold them on the table in either hand. Then you start singing the song and each time you have sung two words you pass the bottles to the person on your right and he will do the same to the person on his right, etc. You do this until you get to the part of the song where it says "with a shovel and a pick and a walking stick." On this part of the song you pick up the two bottles which have been passed to you and instead of passing them on, you move them to your right but bring them back and do this five times (for example every two words). After the word "stick" you once again release the bottles to the person on your right. The song continues going round and mistakes will be made which will obviously result in large drinking fines for all concerned.

100. THREE MAN

This is a game with a number of rules but they are easy to pick up. You need two normal dice and for certain rolls and numbers you are required to do certain commands. If 11 is rolled, then the person next to the thrower drinks. If 7 is rolled, then the person on the other side of the dice thrower drinks. If a 6 and 3 are thrown, then everyone has to put a fist to their cheek and the last to do so drinks a "finger." If 6 and 2 are thrown, then two fingers are put to your cheek and the last person to do so drinks. If a 6 and 1 are thrown, then one finger goes to your cheek and the last man drinks. If the wrong amount of fingers are put against a cheek then the guilty parties automatically drink. You become the "3 Man" if you roll the number 3 or your dice add up to 3 (for example 1+2). Once you are the "3 Man" then every time a 3 is rolled you drink, except if a double 3 is thrown or a 4 and 3. You can only get out of the "3 Man" if you throw a 3. The "3 Man" would then continue to the next person who manages to throw a 3. If a double is thrown, then the thrower may nominate the digits of one of these dice as "fingers" to one or more participants. If, say, double 6 is thrown, then he can give all six "fingers" to one person, or give three "fingers" to two people, etc. Finally you have a "9 Man;" this is when someone rolls 9, they have to drink a "finger" and then the next person in line drinks when the next 9 is thrown. You have to concentrate very hard when playing this game and you must have good luck.

101. Can Crawl

This is an entertaining game to be played at any time during the evening and all you need are two cans. What you do is place your heels against a wall, then crawl out using the cans as your only support to keep you off the ground, and your heels must remain touching the wall throughout. You stretch as far out as you can, place one can down, then try to get back to the wall and stand up without touching the floor and without falling over. The person who gets the can the furthest is the winner and the losers consume four "fingers."

OTHER GREAT BOOKS BY BOSTON AMERICA

The fine cultivated stores carrying our books really get ticked if you buy direct from the publisher so, if you can, please patronize your local store and let them make a buck. If, however, the fools don't carry a particular title, you can order them from us for $8 postpaid. Credit cards accepted for orders of 3 or more books.

#2700 Rules For Sex On Your Wedding Night
All the rules from undressing the bride to ensuring the groom will respect her in the morning.

#2703 You Know You're A Golf Addict When...
You hustle your grandmother, watch golf videos and think you look good in golf clothes.

#2704 What Every Woman Can Learn From Her Cat
You'll learn that an unmade bed is fluffier and there's no problem that can't be helped by a nap among many others.

#2705 Adult Connect The Dots
If you can count to 100 and hold a pencil you can draw really sexy pictures of people doing "you know what".

#2706 Is There Sex After 50?
Everything from swapping for two-25-year olds to finding out it's not sexy tucking your T-shirt into your underpants.

#2707 Beer Is Better Than Women Because...
Beers don't change their minds once you take off their tops and don't expect an hour of foreplay.

#2708 You Know You're Over 30 When...
You start wearing underwear almost all of the time and no longer have to lie on your resume.

#2709 You Know You're Over 40 When...
You feel like the morning after and you can swear you haven't been anywhere and you start to look forward to dull evenings at home.

#2710 You Know You're Over 50 When...
Your arms aren't long enough to hold your reading material and you sit down to put on your underwear.

#2711 You Know You're Over The Hill When...
No one cares any more what you did in high school and you see your old cereal bowl in an antique shop.

#2712 Birthdays Happen
Your biological urges have dwindled to an occasional nudge and you discuss "regularity" at your birthday party.

#2713 Unspeakable Farts
These are the ones that were only whispered about in locker rooms like the "Hold Your Breath Fart" and "The Morning Fart".

#2714 101 Great Drinking Games
A remarkable collection of fun and creative drinking games including all the old favorites and many new ones you can barely imagine.

#2715 How To Have Sex On Your Birthday
Finding a partner, the birthday orgasm, birthday sex games and much more.

#2717 Women Over 40 Are Better Because...
They are smart enough to hire someone to do the cleaning and men at the office actually solicit their advice.

#2718 Women Over 50 Are Better Because...
They don't fall to pieces if you see them without their makeup and are no longer very concerned about being "with it".

#2719 Is There Sex After 40?
Great cartoons analyzing this important subject from sexy cardigans to the bulge that used to be in his trousers.

#2720 Plop
Let's just say this book is a favorite of teenage boys who find the toilet humor about the funniest thing they can imagine.

#2721 Cucumbers Are Better Than Men Because...
They won't make a pass at your friends, don't care if you shave your legs and stay hard for a week.

#2722 Better An Old Fart Than A Young Shithead
A great comparison of the Old Fart who dresses for comfort and the Young Shithead who is afraid of looking like a dork.

#2723 101 Outrageous Things To Do On Your Birthday
Wear a silly hat to work, jump up and down in an elevator, don't wear any underwear and drive straddling 2 lanes.

#2724 My Favorite Teacher
A super gift for a teacher that shows how to handle April Fools Day and outsmart kids who are smarter than the teacher.

#2725 My Favorite Nurse
A gift for nurses that explains how they make doctors look good, eject obnoxious visitors, and keep from getting sick.

#2726 Your New Baby
This is a manual that explains everything from unpacking your new baby to handling kids' plumbing and routine servicing.

#2727 Diddle Your Way To Success With Women
This book teaches how diddling works, basic techniques, first time diddling and how to know when to stop.

#2728 Sex After Retirement
Everyone needs a gift for retiring friends and this riotous cartoon book is perfect to help the retiree while away the hours.

#2729 Great Bachelor Parties
This book tells it all from finding a cooperative stripper to getting rid of the father-in-law to damage control with the bride to be.

#2730 Rules For Engaged Couples
Rules for living together, meeting the family, learning to share and planning the wedding.

#2731 The Bachelorette Party
Great pre-party and party ideas and suggestions for everything from limos to outfits to strippers to your behavior in bars.

#2732 Brides Guide To Sex And Marriage
Dealing with your husband's family and learning what he does in the bathroom and secrets of sleeping comfortably together.

#2403 The Good Bonking Guide
Bonking is a very useful British term for "you know what" and this book covers bonking in the dark, bonking all night long and more.

#2434 Sex And Marriage
Make your wife more exciting in bed and teach your husband about romance. Hobbies, religion and getting a husband to fix your car.

#2501 Cowards Guide To Body Piercing
Cartoons and explanations of all the good and horrible places you can put holes in yourself.

#1500 Fish Tank Video $15 postpaid
This fish tank video enables you to experience all the joys of beautiful, colorful and graceful tropical fish without having to care for them. You'll find yourself hypnotized by the delicate beauty of these fish. Approximately 1 hour running time.

BOSTON AMERICA C★O★R★P

125 Walnut Street, Watertown, MA 02472   (617) 923-1111   FAX: (617) 923-8839